PROPHECY'S DR. JEKYLL AND MR. HYDE

Prophecy's Dr. Jekyll and Mr. Hyde

Stephen Bohr

Remnant
Publications

Coldwater MI 49036
www.remnantpublications.com

Published by
Remnant Publications
649 East Chicago Road
Coldwater MI 49036
517-279-1304
www.remnantpublications.com

The author assumes full responsibility for the accuracy of all facts
and quotations as cited in this book.

Cover design by David Berthiaume
Text design by Greg Solie • AltamontGraphics.com

Library of Congress Cataloging-in-Publication Data

Bohr, Stephen, 1950-
   Prophecy's Dr. Jekyll and Mr. Hyde / by Stephen Bohr.
      p. cm.
   ISBN 978-1-933291-28-4 (alk. paper)
   1. Eschatology. 2. Seventh-Day Adventists--Doctrines. 3. Bible.
O.T. Daniel--Criticism, interpretation, etc. 4. Bible. N.T. Revela-
tion--Criticism, interpretation, etc. I. Title.
   BT821.3.B64 2008
   230'.6732--dc22
                              2008016559

08 09 10 11 12 • 5 4 3 2 1

PROPHECY'S DR. JEKYLL AND MR. HYDE

There is probably no topic that has caused more debate among the leaders of the various churches of the United States in recent years than that of the proper relationship between church and state. Particularly since ministers such as Jerry Falwell and Pat Robertson entered the political arena in the early 1970s, the subject has surfaced time and again.

How should the church relate to the state and the state to the church? Should they be kept totally separate or should they team up as partners in the battle against the encroachments of secular humanism and post-modernism?

In this book I wish to tackle this subject from the perspective of the four gospels, the book of Acts and the books of Daniel and Revelation. The approach will include four main points:

- How Christ and His apostles understood the proper relationship between church and state as found in the Gospels and the book of Acts.

- How the papacy destroyed the understanding of Christ and His apostles.

- How the founding fathers of the United States restored the understanding of Christ and the apostles.

- How, in the near future, apostate Protestantism in the United States will team up with the papacy to destroy the work of the founding fathers.

Let's begin our study by examining the general outline of the remarkable prophecy of Daniel 7.

The Four Beasts of Daniel 7

It has long been recognized by students of Bible prophecy that the four beasts of Daniel 7 represent four consecutive kingdoms that arose in the course of history beginning in the days of king Nebuchadnezzar. History proves that the lion represents the kingdom of Babylon (605–539 B.C.), the bear symbolizes the kingdom of the Medes and Persians (539–331 B.C.), the leopard denotes Greece (331–168 B.C.) and the dragon beast represents Rome.

Four Stages of Rome

What has not received sufficient attention is the fact that the fourth beast (Rome) is described as having four consecutive periods of dominion. These four periods are outlined in Daniel 7:23–27:

Stage #1: The Roman Empire (168 B.C.–A.D. 476)

*"Thus he said: 'The **fourth beast** shall be a **fourth kingdom** on earth, which shall be different from all other kingdoms, and shall devour the whole earth, trample it and break it in pieces."*

Clearly there was a period during which the fourth beast ruled by itself without any horns or divisions. This was the period of what has been called the Iron Monarchy of Rome.

Stage #2: The Divided Roman Empire (A.D. 476–538)

*"The ten horns are ten kings who **shall arise from** this kingdom."*

6

The text is clear. In order for the ten horns to arise **from** this kingdom, the kingdom must have already existed before they arose. History proves that the Roman Empire was carved up and divided among the barbarian tribes who invaded from the north.

Stage #3: Papal Rome during the 1,260 Years (A.D. 538–1798)

*"And another shall rise **after them**; he shall be different from the first ones, and shall subdue three kings. He shall speak **pompous words** against the Most High, shall **persecute** the saints of the Most High, and shall intend to change times and law. Then the saints **shall be given** into his hand for a **time and times and half a time.**"*

The papacy arose among the barbarian kingdoms in Western Europe and ruled over the divided Roman Empire for a period of three and one half prophetic times or 1,260 years.

Stage #4: Papal Rome restored to power sometime after the three and a half times and before the second coming of Jesus

*"'But the court shall be seated, and they shall **take away his** [the little horn's] **dominion**, to **consume and destroy it** forever. Then the kingdom and dominion, and the greatness of the kingdoms under the whole heaven, shall be given to the people, the saints of the Most High. His kingdom is an everlasting kingdom, and all dominions shall serve and obey Him.'"*

7

The fourth stage of the fourth beast is implicit. If the little horn's dominion will be taken away and it will be destroyed when Jesus comes, then it must be ruling the world again at that time. This means that the papacy's career did not end when it lost its dominion at the end of the three and one half prophetic times. It will be alive, well and ruling the world again when Jesus comes and will be destroyed by the brightness of His coming (2 Thessalonians 2:8, 9).

Summarizing the **four stages** of the fourth beast we have:

- *The fourth beast alone: Imperial Rome (168 B.C. –A.D. 476).*

- *The fourth beast with ten horns: Divided Rome (A.D. 476–538).*

- *The fourth beast with the little horn ruling for three and one half prophetic years: Papal Rome's first stage (A.D. 538–1798).*

- *Fourth beast when the little horn is restored to power: Papal Rome's second stage (in the near future).*

Revelation 13:1, 2, 5, 7 Parallels Daniel 7

Even a cursory glance at Revelation 13:1, 2 reveals a clear link with Daniel 7. Notice that the same four beasts are mentioned:

> *"Now the beast which I saw was like a **leopard**, his feet were like the feet of a **bear**, and his mouth like the mouth of a **lion**. The **dragon** gave him his power, his throne, and great authority." Emphasis supplied.*

As with the dragon beast of Daniel 7, the dragon beast of Revelation 12, 13 also has four consecutive stages of dominion:

- **Rome**: *The dragon who sought to kill Jesus (12:1–3).*
- **Divided Rome**: *The dragon had ten horns (12:3).*
- **Papal Rome**: *The beast received its power, throne and great authority from the dragon and ruled for 42 months (13:5).*
- **Papal Rome**: *The beast will rule the world once again after its deadly wound is healed (13:3) .*

It will be noticed that the beast which received its power, its throne and great authority from the dragon performed the **same actions** for the same time period as the little horn:

*"And he was given a **mouth speaking great things** and blasphemies, and he was given authority to continue for **forty-two months**. It was granted to him to make **war with the saints** and to **overcome** them. And authority was given him over every tribe, tongue, and nation." (Revelation 13:5, 7). Emphasis supplied.*

Note of Clarification about the dragon and its ten horns

Someone might ask: Why is the dragon of Revelation 12:3 depicted as having ten horns when Jesus was about to be born if the Roman Empire was not divided until later, in the year 476? The answer is that Revelation 12:3 portrays the total career of the dragon without any distinctions because, as we have seen, Daniel 7:23, 24 has already made those distinctions.

An analogous case can be seen by comparing the four headed leopard beast of Daniel 7 with the four horned he-goat of Daniel 8. In Daniel 7 the four headed leopard represents the Grecian empire in its total career without any distinctions. There is no intimation in Daniel 7 that the leopard ruled for a period before it grew four heads.

Yet we know from Daniel 8 that the leopard did not have the four heads when it rose to power. This is made clear in Daniel 8 where we are told that the he-goat—which is parallel to the leopard—ruled for a period with a notable horn before the other four horns came out.

Daniel's Little Horn and Revelation's Beast

From what we have seen so far it is clear that the beast of Revelation 13:1–10 and the little horn of Daniel 7 represent the same historical power for at least two reasons:

- The **sequence** of powers is the same

  Lion

  Bear

  Leopard

  Dragon

  10 horns

  Little horn/beast rule for 3.5 times or 42 months

  Little horn/beast restored to power

- The **characteristics** of both are also the same.

  They both speak great words against the Most High, they both persecute the saints of the Most High and they both rule for the same time period

The Fourth Stage of the Dragon Beast

It is important to underline that while the fourth stage of the dragon beast was only implied in Daniel 7 it is made explicit in Revelation 13 for we are told there that after the beast ruled for 42 months it will have another period of dominion. In between these two stages the beast is convalescing with a deadly wound.

*"And I saw one of his heads as if it had been **mortally wounded**, and his deadly wound was **healed** and all the world marveled and followed the beast."* *Emphasis supplied.*

Now that we know the chronological sequence of the various stages of the dragon beast's dominion we are ready to focus more specifically on the third and fourth stages of its rule.

Crucial Questions

- With what **weapon** was the beast wounded?
- What does the **sword** represent?
- How and when did the beast **acquire** the sword?
- What is the meaning of the **deadly wound**?
- What keeps the deadly wound **from healing**?
- Was the wound healed in **1801** or **1929**?
- **When** and **how** will the wound be healed and **by whom**?

The Weapon That Wounded the Beast

Revelation 13:10 explains that the deadly wound that ended the dragon's third stage of rule was given with the **sword:**

> "He who leads into captivity shall go into captivity; he who kills **with the sword** must be killed **with the sword.**" Emphasis supplied.

Someone might object: "*The text does not say that the beast killed with the sword and must be killed with the sword; the text uses the indefinite: 'he who.'*"

But Revelation 13:14 leaves no doubt that it was the beast who killed with the sword and in turn was killed with it:

> "And he deceives those who dwell on the earth by those signs which he was granted to do in the sight of the beast, telling those who dwell on the earth to make an image to **the beast who was wounded by the sword** and lived." Emphasis supplied.

What Is Represented by a Sword?

Whenever I ask this question in my prophecy lectures, the answer invariably comes back: '*The sword represents the Word of God.*' And this is true, but not always. Let's notice **Ephesians 6:17:**

> "And take the helmet of salvation, and the **sword of the Spirit**, which is the **word of God.**" Emphasis supplied.

The sword of the Spirit is given to the church and she uses it when she preaches the Word of God through the ministration of the Holy Spirit (see Romans 10:17; Hebrews 4:12, 13). In the hand of the church this sword persuades, it does not coerce; it is redemptive, not punitive. Everyone is free to accept or reject its testimony. If someone hears this Word and teaches or lives contrary to it he can be excommunicated from the fellowship of the church in the present and that very Word will judge and punish him at the **last day** (John 12:48; Revelation 19:15).

The Sword That Wounded the Beast

It goes without saying that this cannot be the sword that wounded the beast at the end of the 1,260 years because we are told explicitly that the **very sword** that the beast used to kill the saints during the 1,260 years would be used to kill it at the end of this period.

It is rather obvious that the papacy did not use the Bible during the 1,260 years to kill dissenters (rather it forbade the Bible!) so the symbol of the sword in the context of Revelation 13 must represent something different than in Ephesians 6:17.

The crucial question is this: Which sword did the papacy use to persecute God's saints during its period of supremacy? The answer is found in Romans 13:1–4:

> *"Let every soul be subject to the **governing authorities**. For there is no authority except from God, and the **authorities** that exist are appointed by God. Therefore whoever resists the **authority** resists the ordinance of God and those who resist will bring judgment on themselves. For **rulers** are not a terror to good works but to evil. Do you want to be unafraid of the **authority**? Do what is good, and you will have praise from the same. For he is God's minister to you for good. But if you do evil, be afraid; for he does not bear **the sword** in vain; for he is God's minister, an **avenger to execute wrath** on him who practices evil." Emphasis supplied.*

In the Bible, symbols are flexible. That is to say, they do not always mean the same thing—the context must dictate their meaning. The sword that is mentioned in Romans 13 threatens **civil penalties** against transgressors. These verses make it crystal clear that this sword is in the hand of the ruling authorities and magistrates. It does not belong to the **church** but rather to the **state**. This sword is punitive, not redemptive. It punishes violations of civil law with civil penalties.

It is important to realize that God has established both church and state. In God's order they both have their legitimate place and function.

In Matthew 16:16 Jesus announced to Peter that He would build His church upon the Rock, that is, Himself. Thus Christ predicted the establishment of His spiritual kingdom.

But Romans 13 also makes it very clear that the state was established by God—it is even called God's minister. But the state is God's minister to punish violations of civil law, not religious law. Romans 13 explicitly affirms that the state is God's minister to preserve the civil order of society. In the days when Paul wrote this sword was in the hand of the Roman Empire.

Remarkably, Jesus refused to allow His followers (the incipient church of that age) to use the temporal sword to defend His kingdom.

When the mob came to arrest Jesus in the Garden of Gethsemane we are told that Peter drew his sword and cut off the ear of the high priest's servant. Peter, who was supposedly the first pope, was using the **temporal** sword to defend His Master's **spiritual** kingdom.

Did Jesus encourage such behavior? Did he commend Peter for using the literal sword to defend His kingdom? Did He rebuke His other disciples for not following Peter's laudable example? Absolutely not! Jesus soundly rebuked Peter in words strikingly similar to those of Revelation 13:10:

"But Jesus said to him, 'Put your sword in its place, for all who **take the sword** will **perish by the sword.**" (Matthew 26:52). Emphasis supplied.

A few hours later when Pilate asked Jesus if He was a king Jesus promptly replied:

"My kingdom is **not of this world**. If My kingdom were of this world, My **servants would fight**, so that I should not be delivered to the Jews; but now My kingdom is **not from here**." (John 18:36). Emphasis supplied.

Jesus refused to allow His followers to employ the temporal sword to establish or to defend His spiritual kingdom.

What Is the Deadly Wound?

Now that we know that the sword of Revelation 13:10 represents the punitive power of the state to enforce civil laws upon transgressors, we must seek to discover what is meant by the deadly wound.

A careful study of Revelation 13:10 reveals that the deadly wound does not refer primarily to the confiscation of the territories of the Roman Catholic Church. Neither is it the elimination of the Roman Catholic Church as a church.

The deadly wound was given to the papacy when the sword of the state that the papacy had used to persecute God's people during the 1,260 years turned against it. The deadly wound then was the removal of the sword of the state from the hand of the papacy.

How Did the Papacy Obtain the Sword?

Between the year 300 and the year 476 hordes of barbarian tribes from the north invaded and carved up the Roman Empire. The last emperor was Romulus Augustulus who was deposed in the year 476. The barbarian incursions into the Roman Empire turned it upside down and left it without a civil ruler who could preserve law and order. In the midst of this chaotic situation, the Bishop of Rome took the reigns of civil power. He was now not only the spiritual leader of the church but also the temporal ruler of the state.

Cardinal **Edward Manning** described the manner in which the Roman Pontiff originally gained his power. When the barbarians invaded the Roman Empire and tore it apart Manning explains that:

> *"The pontiffs found themselves alone, the sole fountains of order, peace, law, and safety. And from the hour of this providential **liberation**, when, by a divine intervention, the **chains fell off** from the hands of the successor of St. Peter, as once before from his own, no sovereign has ever reigned in Rome except the Vicar of Jesus Christ." Henry Edward Manning, The Temporal Power of the Vicar of Jesus Christ, Preface, pp. xxviii, xxix. (London: Burns and Lambert, 1862). Emphasis supplied.*

Manning further explains:

> *"It [the papacy] waited until such a time as God should break its **bonds** asunder, and **should liberate it from subjection to civil powers,** and **enthrone it** in the possession of a temporal sovereignty of its own." Henry Edward Manning, The Temporal Power of the Vicar of*

Jesus Christ (London: Burns & Lambert, second edi-
tion, 1862), pp. 11–13. Emphasis supplied.

Manning is saying that when the civil power of Rome
was removed by the barbarians, the bishop of Rome filled the
vacuum and became the arbiter in civil affairs as well as in
spiritual. Remarkably, Manning refers to this taking over of
civil power by the bishop of Rome with expressions such as
"*breaking bonds asunder*", and "*chains falling off.*"

In cryptic language, the apostle Paul had already referred
to this removal of the civil power from the Roman Empire
when he wrote about the removal of the mysterious restrain-
er of 2 Thessalonians 2:6, 7:

> "And now you know what is **restraining** [the civil pow-
> er of the Roman Empire], that he [the antichrist] may
> be revealed in his own time. For the mystery of lawless-
> ness is already at work; only He who **now restrains**
> [the emperor] will do so until He is **taken out of the
> way** [by the barbarian invasions]." Emphasis supplied.

Another Roman Catholic theologian affirms:

> "Long ages ago, when Rome through the neglect of the
> Western emperors was left to the mercy of the barba-
> rous hordes, the Romans turned to one figure for aid
> and protection, and **asked him to rule them**; and thus,
> in this simple manner, the best title of all to kingly right,
> commenced the **temporal sovereignty of the popes**.
> And meekly stepping to the **throne of Caesar**, the Vicar
> of Christ **took up the scepter** to which the emperors
> and kings of Europe were to **bow in reverence** through
> so many ages." James P. Conroy, <u>American Catholic
> Quarterly Review</u>, April, 1911. Emphasis supplied.

Scores of church historians have said the same:

*"Under the Roman Empire [stage # 1] the popes had no temporal powers. But when the Roman Empire had disintegrated and its place had been taken by a number of rude, barbarous kingdoms [stage # 2], the Roman Catholic Church not only became independent of the states in religious affairs but dominated **secular affairs** as well [stage # 3]." Carl Conrad Eckhardt, The Papacy and World Affairs (Chicago: The University of Chicago Press, 1937), p. 1. Emphasis supplied.*

Though Eckhardt is probably not aware of it, he is fitly describing the first three stages of the dragon beast of Daniel 7 and Revelation 12 and 13.

Church historian, R. W. Southern further explains the relationship between the papacy and the state during the middle ages:

*"During the whole medieval period there was **in Rome a single spiritual and temporal authority** [the papacy] exercising powers which in the end exceeded those that had ever lain within the grasp of the Roman emperor." R. W. Southern, Western Society and the Church in the Middle Ages, vol 2, pp. 24–25. Emphasis supplied.*

John N. Figgis adds his testimony:

*"[In] the Middle Ages the church was not a State, it was the State; or rather, the civil authority (for a separate society was not recognized), was merely the **police department** of the Church..." John N. Figgis, From Gerson to Grotius, p. 4. Emphasis supplied.*

This idea of the church ruling in temporal as well as in spiritual affairs was originally suggested by Augustine and later developed by popes Gregory VII and Innocent III. It was finally fleshed out in 1302 when pope Boniface VIII wrote a significant bull (personal letter) titled <u>Unam Sanctam</u>. In this letter Boniface developed a theological idea that had originally been proposed by St. Bernard in which he spoke about the two swords:

> "We are informed by the texts of the gospels that in this [Roman Catholic] Church and in its power are **two swords**; namely, the spiritual and the temporal. **Both, therefore, are in the power of the Church**, that is to say, the spiritual and the material sword, but the former [the spiritual] is to be administered for the Church but the latter [the temporal] by the Church; the former in the hands of the priest; the latter by the hands of kings and soldiers, but **at the will and sufferance of the priest**." Emphasis supplied.

What Happened in 1798?

The year 1798 marked the climax of the French Revolution that began in 1793. The Revolution was an uprising against both kingly power and priestly intolerance. On February 12, 1798 general Berthier entered Vatican City, deposed pope Pius VI, informed him that his power was at an end, and took him prisoner to France where he later died in exile. The emperor, Napoleon Bonaparte, had already given the order that a successor not be elected.

It is interesting to note how historians describe the deadly wound of 1798. They employ language very similar to that of Revelation 13. Let's take a few examples.

*"The papacy was **extinct; not a vestige of its existence remained**; and among all the Roman Catholic powers **not a finger was stirred** in its defense [because it no longer had the support of the state]. The Eternal City had no longer prince or pontiff; its bishop was a dying captive in foreign lands; and the decree was already announced that **no successor** would be allowed in its place." George Trevor, Rome: From the Fall of the Western Empire pp. 439, 440. Emphasis supplied.*

*"No wonder that half of Europe thought Napoleon's veto would be obeyed, and that with the Pope the **Papacy was dead.**" Joseph Rickaby, Lectures on the History of Religion, 'The Modern Papacy,' volume 3, p. 1. Emphasis supplied.*

*"Multitudes imagined that **the papacy was at the point of death** and asked, would Pius VI be the last pontiff, and if the close of the eighteenth century would be signalized by the fall of the papal dynasty." T. H. Gill, The Papal Drama, book 10. Emphasis supplied.*

*"... the Papacy had suffered its deepest humiliation... [and] appeared to be **annihilated** ... The Revolution also dealt it the **wound** which, it seemed did not want to **heal** until **far into** the twentieth century." (**M. Weitlauff**, quoted in, Frank B. Holbrook, Symposium on Revelation, volume 2 (Hagerstown, Maryland: Review and Herald, 1992), p. 337. Emphasis supplied.*

*"The object of the French directory was the **destruction of the pontifical government**, as the irreconcilable enemy of the republic. ... The aged pope [Pius VI] was summoned to **surrender the temporal government**;*

on his refusal, he was dragged from the altar. ... His rings were torn from his fingers, and finally, after declaring **the temporal power abolished***, the victors carried the pope prisoner into Tuscany, whence he never returned (1798). George Trevor,* Rome: From the Fall of the Western Empire *(London: The Religious Tract Society, 1868), pp. 439, 440. Emphasis supplied.*

One can't help but sense the irony of what took place in 1798. France is known as the eldest daughter of the papacy because Clovis, king of the Franks, was the first who officially gave temporal power to the papacy in the year 508. Strikingly, the very nation that had first given the papacy the sword, now turned on her mother and gave her the deadly wound.

The French Revolution was a catastrophic event for the papacy. In the aftermath of the Revolution country after country in the western world followed the example of France and the United States establishing democratic governments that proclaimed their emancipation from the straightjacket of the papacy. But though the Revolution well nigh annihilated the papacy, prophecy foretells that she will arise from her deathbed far more powerful and despotic than in the past.

The Healing of the Wound

Revelation 13:3 describes the healing of the papacy's deadly wound:

"And I saw one of his heads as if it had been **mortally wounded***, and his deadly wound was* **healed** *and all the world marveled and followed the beast." Emphasis supplied.*

21

What is the healing of the papacy's deadly wound? Is it primarily the restoration of her confiscated territory? Is it the recovery of her ecclesiastical power? Not really.

You see the term 'papacy' is a code word for a religious-political system that employs the power of the state to compel people to obey its dictates. In other words the papacy is not merely a church but an amalgamation of church and state.

If the deadly wound means that the state turned against the papacy and took away the sword from her in 1798, then the healing of the wound must mean that the state will once again give back to her the power of the sword that she lost in that year. Ellen White described the papacy's ardent desire to recover what she lost in 1798:

> "But Romanism as a system is no more in harmony with the gospel of Christ now than at any former period in her history. The Protestant churches are in great darkness, or they would discern the signs of the times. The Roman Church is far-reaching in her plans and modes of operation. She is employing every device to extend her influence and increase her power in preparation for a fierce and determined conflict to **regain** control of the world, to **re-establish** persecution, and to **undo** all that Protestantism has done." The Great Controversy, pp. 565, 566. Emphasis supplied.

The words 'regain' and 'reestablish' bring to mind the fact that the papacy lost control of the world when the sword of the state was removed from her hand and turned against her in 1798. Since then she has not been able to persecute as she did in her heyday.

Was the Deadly Wound Healed in 1801?

It is a little known fact in Adventist circles that a new pope was elected just three and a half years after the deadly wound was given in February of 1798. Not only was a new pope elected but he was even allowed to retain possession of his Italian principality. Says historian Arthur Robert Pennington:

> *"He [Napoleon] felt that, as the large majority of the inhabitants of France knew no other form of faith than Romanism, it must become the **established religion of the country**. Accordingly we find that he now began negotiations with the Pope, which issued in a Concordat in July, 1801, whereby the Roman Catholic religion was once more **established in France**. He also left Pius in **possession of his Italian principality**."* Arthur Robert Pennington, <u>Epochs</u> <u>of</u> <u>the</u> <u>Papacy</u>, pp. 450, 452. Emphasis supplied.

There are strong reasons to believe that the deadly wound was not healed in 1801. What are they?

First of all, as we shall see in due course, prophecy clearly indicates that the United States will be the power that will restore the sword to the papacy, **not France**.

Secondly, even though the papacy retained its territory and principality, the nations of Europe wanted nothing to do with her. Europe did not wonder after the beast or worship it, much less the world.

This helplessness of the papacy is revealed in a book written by Cardinal Edward Manning and published in 1862 where he rebukes the nations of Europe for forsaking the papacy:

> *"See this Catholic Church, this Church of God, feeble and weak, rejected even by the **very nations called**

Catholic. *There is Catholic* **France**, *and Catholic* **Germany**, *and Catholic* **Italy** *giving up this exploded figment of the* **temporal power** *of the Vicar of Jesus Christ.' And so, because the Church* **seems weak**, *and the Vicar of the Son of God is renewing the Passion of his Master upon earth, therefore we are scandalized, therefore we* **turn our faces from him**." *The Temporal Power of the Vicar of Jesus Christ, pp. 140, 141. Emphasis supplied.*

Third, the nations of Europe did not erect an **image** to the beast nor did they enforce the **mark** of the beast after the concordat of 1801.

Finally, the power of the papacy was severely restricted by the French government. The state elected the bishops and paid the clergy and the clergy were required to swear an oath of allegiance to the state.

This leads us to conclude that the recovery of spiritual dominion and territory does not necessarily mean that the deadly wound was healed.

The Wound of 1870

Another little known fact in Adventist circles is that the papacy received a further wound on September 20, 1870 when King Victor Emmanuel II confiscated the Papal States and united Italy. As a result the papacy lost most of its territory (except for a handful of buildings in Vatican City). In protest, Pope Pius IX and his successors declared themselves prisoners of the Vatican and as a result no pope left Vatican City for the next 59 years.

During his pontificate of 46 years Pope Pius IX further alienated and angered the governments of western Europe and the United States by proclaiming the *Dogma of the*

Immaculate Conception [1854] by publishing his *Syllabus of Errors* where he railed against democratic governments and civil and religious liberty [1864] and by convoking Vatican Council I where the embarrassing *Dogma of Papal Infallibility* [1870] was proclaimed. This takes us to the year 1929.

Was the Deadly Wound Healed in 1929?

Much has been made of the year 1929 by some Adventist writers. Was the deadly wound really healed in that year? There are several convincing reasons why we cannot say that the wound was healed in 1929. Let's examine them.

First of all, the concordat that was signed between the papacy and the Italian government in 1929 had to do with the wound the papacy received in **1870** and not the one it received in 1798.

Secondly, the book of Revelation makes it clear as we shall see that the United States, **not Italy,** would be the nation to bring about the healing of the wound.

Even more significantly, the whole world did not wonder after the papacy nor was an image of and to it erected nor was its mark enforced as a result of what happened in 1929.

Where, then, did many Adventists get the idea that the wound was healed in 1929? The answer is found in an article that appeared in the San Francisco Chronicle the very day that the 1929 Concordat was signed.

The headline on the front-page of the newspaper read:

*"VATICAN AGAIN AT PEACE WITH
ITALY AFTER LONG QUARREL"*

In smaller lettering appeared the words:

"Heal Wound of Many Years."

The part of the article that was most significant to Adventists was this:

"The Roman question tonight was a thing of the past and the Vatican was at peace with Italy. The formal accomplishment of this today was the exchange of signatures in the historic Palace of St. John Lateran by two noteworthy plenipotentiaries, Cardinal Gasparri for Pope Pius XI and Premier Mussolini for King Victor Emmanuel III.

*"In affixing the autographs to the memorable document, **healing the wound** which has festered **since 1870** [not since 1798], extreme cordiality was displayed on both sides." The San Francisco Chronicle, February 11, 1929, p. 1. Emphasis supplied.*

The *New York Times* reported on this important event:

*"The Pope is again an **independent sovereign ruler**, as he was throughout the middle Ages, though his temporal realm, established today, is the most microscopic independent State in the world, and probably the smallest in all history." The New York Times, Tuesday, February 12, 1929. Emphasis supplied.*

The article in the *San Francisco Chronicle* makes it abundantly clear that the wound that was healed in 1929 was the one given the papacy in 1870 and not the one she received in 1798.

Don't get me wrong. What happened in 1929 was very significant. The recovery of temporal sovereignty by the papacy was an important occurrence. We might go so far as to say that the wounds of the papacy began to be healed in that year. But the wound was not **healed** in that year. in order for the wound to be healed, the secular powers of the world must give her back the sword.

Why Hasn't the Mortal Wound Healed Yet?

The late Malachi Martin the Jesuit exorcist of the Roman Catholic Church and author of the best selling book, The Keys of This Blood, said in 1986:

> *"[For] **fifteen hundred years** and more, Rome had kept as strong a hand as possible in each local community around the wide world. ... By and large, and admitting some exceptions, that had been the Roman view until* ***two hundred years of inactivity*** *had been* ***imposed*** *upon the papacy by the* ***major secular powers of the world.***" *Quoted in* Christianity Today, *November 21, 1986, p. 26. Emphasis supplied.*

There are several remarkable things about this statement that we must dwell upon.

First, if we go backward in time about two hundred years from 1986 we arrive at around the time of the French Revolution. Although Malachi Martin obviously did not believe that the deadly wound of Revelation 13 applies to the papacy, nevertheless he was tacitly admitting that the French Revolution brought into existence **secular democratic governments** that have kept the papacy in a straightjacket for the last two hundred years. As we have seen, this is the meaning of the deadly wound.

Second, Malachi Martin is explicitly admitting that as of 1986 the papacy had not yet recovered the power she lost during the French Revolution. In other words, Martin was inadvertently saying that the wound was not healed in 1929.

Ellen White concurred with Martin although she wrote a hundred years earlier:

> "Let the **restraints** now imposed by **secular govern-
> ments** be removed and Rome be **reinstated** in her for-
> mer power, and there would speedily be a **revival** of
> her tyranny and persecution. The Great Controversy,
> p. 564. Emphasis supplied._

Ellen White's use of the words "*reinstated*" and "*revival*"
indicates that the papacy's deadly wound will be healed when
the secular governments remove their restraints.

The reason why the mortal wound has not yet healed is
because the secular governments of the world have not allowed the papacy to ride on them once again. So to speak,
the chains that fell off the hands of the papacy when the civil
power of the Roman Empire fell in the third and fourth centuries were slapped back on her hands in 1798.

Perhaps this is what is meant by the expression '*he who
leads into captivity will go into captivity.*' Ellen White, more
than one hundred years ago, described the present helplessness of the papacy and her aspirations to global power and
control:

> "*Rome is aiming to **re-establish** her power, to **re-
> cover** her lost supremacy. Let the principle once be
> established in the United States that the **church may
> employ or control the power of the state**; that reli-
> gious observances may be **enforced by secular laws**;
> in short, that the authority of **church and state** is to
> dominate the conscience and the triumph of Rome in
> this country is assured.*" The Great Controversy, p. 581.
> Emphasis supplied.

It is clear that if Rome needs to **reestablish** and **recover**
her **lost** supremacy, she must have been a wounded power
when Ellen White wrote. It will be noticed that the author

also makes it crystal clear that the United States will be the nation instrumental in the healing of the deadly wound.

John W. Robbins, a Reformed theologian, quotes Ayn Rand approvingly as he agrees with both Malachi Martin and Ellen White:

> *"Ayn Rand was right when she wrote in 1967: 'The Catholic Church has never given up the hope to re-establish [she must have once had it and lost it] the medieval union of church and state, with a global state and a global theocracy as its ultimate goal.' The Roman Church-State is a hybrid—a monster of ecclesiastical and political power. Its political thought is totalitarian, and whenever it has had the opportunity to apply its principles, the result has been bloody repression. If, during the last 30 years, it has softened its assertions of full, supreme, and irresponsible power, and has murdered fewer people than before, such changes in behavior are not due to a change in its ideas, but to a change in its circumstances [the secular governments keep her at arms' length] ... The Roman Church-State in the twentieth century, however, is an institution recovering from a mortal wound. If and when it regains [so it must have lost it] its full power and authority, it will impose a regime more sinister than any the planet has yet seen [the deadly wound will be healed]."* John W. Robbins, Ecclesiastical Megalomania, p. 195. Emphasis supplied.

In his book The Keys of This Blood, Malachi Martin described the competition for global control among **three systems**: Capitalism, Communism, and Roman Catholicism:

"There is one great similarity shared by all three of these globalist competitors. Each one has in mind a particular grand design for one world governance ... Their geopolitical competition is about which of the three will form, dominate and run the world system that will replace the decaying nation system." Malachi Martin, The Keys of This Blood, p. 18)

Martin harbors no doubts about who will win in this tooth and nail competition—the Roman Catholic papacy. And Martin describes in chilling words what will happen when the papacy regains its power:

"No holds barred because, once the competition has been decided, the world and all that's in it—our way of life as individuals and as citizens of the nations; our families and our jobs; our trade and commerce and money; our educational systems and our religions and our cultures; even the badges of our national identity, which most of us have always taken for granted—all will have been powerfully and radically altered forever. No one can be exempted from its effects. No sector of our lives will remain untouched. ... Nobody who is acquainted with the plans of these three rivals has any doubt but that only one of them can win" Malachi Martin, The Keys of This Blood, p. 16.

And what is the time frame for this geopolitical New World Order under the leadership of the Roman Catholic papacy?

"As to the time factor involved, those of us who are under seventy will see at least the basic structures of the new world government installed. Those of us under

forty will surely live under its legislative, executive and judiciary authority and control." Malachi Martin, The Keys of This Blood, pp. 15, 16.

The Healing of the Wound

The crucial question is this: How will the papacy regain the power of the sword that it lost over two hundred years ago? Who will loose the chains that have restrained this system for the last two centuries? Even more pointedly, what nation in the world would be foolish enough to place the sword once again in the hand of such a despotic power?

Prophecy reveals that the sword of civil power will be restored to the papacy with the aid of the most unlikely of nations.

The Beast from the Earth

Revelation 13:11 describes a two horned beast that rises from the earth who will compel the entire world to worship the beast that was wounded with the sword. It will set up an image of and to it and will impose its mark. This two-horned beast will be the sword in the hand of the papacy and we are told that it will kill with that sword everyone who dissents:

"He [the two-horned beast] was granted power to give breath to the image of the beast, that the image of the beast should both speak and cause as many as would not worship the image of the beast to be killed." (Revelation 13:15). Emphasis supplied.

In Revelation 13:11 we find a description of this land beast:

*"Then I saw another beast coming up out of the earth, and he had **two horns** like a **lamb** and spoke like a **dragon**."* Emphasis supplied.

What's remarkable about this beast is its split personality. It has two horns like a lamb but at the same time it speaks like a dragon. Notably, the two horns are not broken off before it begins to speak like a dragon. It speaks like a dragon while it still continues to have the two lamblike horns on its head. The character of this beast is reminiscent of the split personality manifested by Dr Jekyll (good) and Mr. Hyde (evil).

The Identity of the Dragon

An important question is this: What is meant by the fact that the beast with lamblike horns speaks like a dragon? In order to answer this question we must understand what the dragon represents.

In the book of Revelation the dragon primarily represents Satan (Revelation 12:7–9) but it also symbolizes **Rome** in its various stages.

It was Satan who stood next to the woman to devour her child as soon as he was born but Satan operated through the instrumentality of Herod, a civil ruler of the Roman Empire (Revelation 12:3 [Daniel 7:23] Matthew 2:16).

When Imperial Rome disintegrated, we are told that it gave its seat, its power and its great authority to the beast (Revelation 13:2). That is to say, the papacy continued to exercise the powers of the dragon—Satan and Rome.

Thus when we are told in Revelation 13:11 that the beast from the earth will speak like a dragon it must mean that this beast will not only be a spokesman for Satan but also for Rome. And so, the dragon, the sea beast and the land beast are all agents of Satan who operates through Rome.

This phenomenon of Satan operating through Rome can be clearly discerned in Revelation 12. It was the dragon—Satan through pagan Rome—who attempted to kill the child (Revelation 12:1-5). It was the dragon—Satan through papal Rome—who persecuted the woman for 1,260 years (Revelation 12:6, 13-15) and it will be the dragon—Satan through resurrected papal Rome with the aid of apostate Protestantism—who will persecute the remnant of the woman's seed when the deadly wound is healed (Revelation 12:17). This is the reason why Revelation 13:4 says that the world will not only worship the beast but it will also worship the dragon from whom the beast received its power, its throne and great authority!

A Unique Beast

In Bible prophecy each successive beast conquered and destroyed the previous one. But this lamb horned beast is different. It is the only beast in prophecy that actually helps the previous beast to recover its lost power. Furthermore, this is the only time in Bible prophecy where we are explicitly told what kind of horns a beast had on its head—lamblike horns.

A Beast Represents a Nation or Empire

It is universally agreed among students of apocalyptic prophecy that beasts symbolize or represent kingdoms. In the book of Daniel, the lion, the bear, the leopard, the dragon, the ram and the he-goat all represent nations or kingdoms.

The noted Bible commentator, **Adam Clarke** wisely remarked about this lamb-horned beast:

*"As a beast has already been shown to be the **symbol of a kingdom** or empire, the rising up of this second*

*beast must consequently represent the rising up of
another empire." Emphasis supplied.*

Two Kingdoms Within One Nation

Adam Clarke also correctly explained that the two horns
of the land beast represent kingdoms:

*"As the seven-headed beast is represented as having
ten horns, which signify so many kingdoms leagued together to support the Latin Church, so the beast which
rises out of the earth has also two horns, which **must
consequently represent two kingdoms**; for if horns of
a beast mean kingdoms in one part of the Apocalypse,
kingdoms must be intended by this symbol whenever it
is used in a similar way in any other part of this book."
Emphasis supplied.*

Was Adam Clarke correct in his assessment? I believe
we can prove that he was. The closest biblical parallel to the
lamb-horned beast of Revelation 13:11 is the ram of Daniel
8. Let's notice verses three and twenty:

*"Then I lifted my eyes and saw, and there, standing be-
side the river, was a **ram** which had **two horns**, and the
two horns were high; but one was higher than the other, and the higher one came up last... The ram which
you saw, having the two horns—they are the **kings of
Media and Persia**." Emphasis supplied.*

It will be noticed that the ram represents **one** nation
composed of **dual** kingdoms—the Medes and the Persians.
The inevitable conclusion is that the two horns like a lamb in
Revelation 13:11 symbolize two kingdoms that exist side by
side within a single nation.

Why the Horns Are Lamblike

The word 'Lamb' appears twenty-nine times in the book of Revelation. In twenty-eight of the twenty-nine times it appears it refers indisputably to Christ. But, does it also apply to Christ in this case?

The text of Revelation 13:11 strongly suggests that the two lamblike horns are in antithesis to the dragon's voice. The Greek conjunction *kai* ('and') is used in various ways in the New Testament. In the book of Revelation it can mean 'and' but it can also mean 'yet' or 'but.' This land beast has two horns like a lamb **and yet** (or but) it speaks like a dragon. Thayer's Greek Lexicon explains one of the meanings of the conjunction *kai:* "with a certain rhetorical emphasis, it annexes something apparently at variance with what has been previously said *and yet.*"

Thus the sense of the text can mean that the two-horned beast has two horns like a lamb and **at the same time** it speaks like a dragon or it can mean that it has two horns like a lamb and **yet** it speaks as a dragon. The text seems to include both meanings. The New International Version translates: *"He had two horns like a lamb,* **but** *he spoke as a dragon."* On the other hand the New King James (as well as other translations) translates: *"he had two horns like a lamb* **and** *spoke like a dragon."*

It is clear from Revelation 13:11 that the two horns like a lamb constitute the positive or favorable side of the land beast while the dragon's voice is the negative side. That is to say, it professes to believe in the two kingdoms that Jesus believed in but at the same time it contradicts its profession in actual practice. In Revelation Jesus is consistently described as being in conflict with the dragon but here the beast with lamblike horns and the dragon appear to be collaborators.

Being that the two horns represent kingdoms that Jesus sanctioned, the question is: Which two kingdoms did Jesus, the Lamb, recognize? Before we answer this question, let's summarize what we have studied so far about this beast.

Conclusion and Summary:
The land beast represents a single **nation**. The two lamblike horns represent the fact that this one nation is composed of **dual kingdoms**. The horns are lamblike so they must represent two kingdoms that were **taught** and **recognized** by **Jesus.**

What Two Kingdoms Did Jesus Sanction?
Now we must ask the question: Which two kingdoms did Jesus, the Lamb, explicitly believe in and teach about?

Let's go to Matthew 22:15–21 for the unequivocal answer:

*"Then the Pharisees went and plotted how they might entangle Him in His talk. And they sent to Him their disciples with the Herodians, saying, "Teacher, we know that You are true, and teach the way of God in truth; nor do You care about anyone, for You do not regard the person of men. Tell us, therefore, what do You think? Is it lawful to pay taxes to Caesar, or not?" But Jesus perceived their wickedness, and said, "Why do you test Me, you hypocrites? Show Me the tax money." So they brought Him a denarius. And He said to them, "Whose image and inscription is this?" They said to Him, "Caesar's." And He said to them, "Render therefore to **Caesar** the things that are Caesar's, and to **God** the things that are God's."*

This passage underlines the fact that Jesus believed in and taught the existence of **two separate kingdoms**. One belonged to God (the church) and the other belonged to Caesar (the state), but they both existed side by side in the one Roman Empire. Jesus was saying that we have financial obligations to both kingdoms. To Caesar we owe our taxes and to God we owe His tithe.

Shortly after His baptism Jesus was led by the Spirit to the wilderness to be tempted of the devil. Though the first two temptations were powerful, the last was the most enticing:

> *"Again, the devil took Him up on an exceedingly high mountain, and showed Him **all the kingdoms of the world and their glory**. And he said to Him, "All these things I will give You if You will fall down and worship me." (Matthew 4:8, 9). Emphasis supplied.*

The response of Jesus to this offer of power and riches was immediate and decisive:

> *Then Jesus said to him, "Away with you, Satan! For it is written, 'You shall worship the LORD your God, and Him only you shall serve.' "(Matthew 4:10)*

If Jesus had accepted the kingdoms of this world and their glory He would have become the vice-regent or associate of Satan. But Jesus refused to be the king of this world because His kingdom was a spiritual one from above.

Jesus knew that His kingdom would conquer the world through the "foolishness of preaching" and not through the use of political maneuvering and the force of arms.

In the third and fourth centuries Satan offered the bishop of Rome those same kingdoms with all their glory and he gladly accepted them. In this way he became the vice-regent of Satan.

This temptation on the Mount was not the only time that Satan attempted to entice Jesus to accept the kingdoms of this world.

In John 6 we find Jesus feeding a crowd of five thousand men with just five loaves and two fishes. When the populace saw this spectacular sign, they immediately believed that He was the long expected Messiah and took measures to make Him their king (John 6:14, 15). But Jesus showed no interest whatsoever in their proposal. He withdrew to a quiet and desolate place to commune with His Father.

Notably, the Jews followed Jesus for three **wrong** reasons. First, because of the miracles he performed on the sick (John 6:1, 2); second, because He brought material prosperity (John 6:26, 27); and third, because they wanted Him to assert political power as their Messiah (John 6:15). They had no interest in the mysterious spiritual kingdom that Jesus offered them as can be seen later on in the story. When Jesus explained that they must assimilate His Word and in this way they would partake of His life, they left deeply disappointed. They wanted worldly prosperity, signs and wonders, and political power and Jesus seemed like the quickest and easiest way to acquire them.

The disciples of Jesus were not immune from this desire for a political Messiah. Two of His disciples, James and John the Sons of Thunder, requested that Jesus give them the two highest places of power and prosperity in the kingdom they soon expected Jesus to establish. The fact that the other disciples were angered by this request shows that they too aspired to these elevated positions. Jesus explained to them that the highest position of honor and power is found in being a servant (Mark 10:35–45).

These same Sons of Thunder also revealed how they expected to establish the kingdom of Jesus (see John 9:51ff). On His last journey to Jerusalem Jesus sent messengers ahead of Him to a Samaritan village to prepare the way. When the village refused to allow Jesus to pass through, James and John were indignant and asked Jesus if He wanted them to bring fire down from heaven to incinerate them. They were determined to destroy by force all those who did not accept Jesus and His kingdom. But Jesus answered them:

> *"You do not know what manner of spirit you are of. For the Son of Man did not come to destroy men's lives but to save them." (Luke 9:55, 56).*

Later on in His ministry Jesus explained the nature of His kingdom:

> *"Now when He was asked by the Pharisees when the kingdom of God would come, He answered them and said, "The kingdom of God does not come with observation [with external display]; nor will they say, 'See here!' or 'See there!' For indeed* **the kingdom of God is within you."** *(Luke 17:20, 21). Emphasis supplied.*

In a private conversation between Jesus and Pilate we once more see that Jesus believed in the existence of two kingdoms within the Roman Empire but separate one from the other. When Pilate asked Jesus during His trial if He was a king Jesus affirmed that He indeed was but then He stated:

> *"My* **kingdom** *is not of* **this world.** *If* **My kingdom** *were of this world, My servants* **would fight,** *so that I should not be delivered to the Jews; but now My* **kingdom** *is not from here." (John 18:36). Emphasis supplied.*

Here Jesus explicitly affirmed that His followers are not to use the temporal sword to defend His kingdom. His kingdom does not involve fighting with the physical sword; His kingdom conquers the world by the preaching of the gospel through the power of the Holy Spirit.

This became patently clear later on in the book of Acts. Just ten days before the outpouring of the Holy Spirit, the disciples were once again thinking about the establishment of Christ's temporal kingdom on earth (Acts 1:6). But Jesus told them:

> *"But you shall receive power when the Holy Spirit has come upon you; and you shall be witnesses to Me in Jerusalem, and in all Judea and Samaria, and to the end of the earth." (Acts 1:8).*

The ten days in the Upper Room changed the focus of the disciples. They finally understood that the kingdom of Christ would be established by the preaching of the Word (the spiritual sword) in the whole world through the power of the Holy Spirit. Satan's kingdom would not be overcome by the love of force but rather by the force of love.

From Acts 2 onward we find no evidence of an entanglement of the apostles with the state. We never find them using the weapons of the state to accomplish the task of converting subjects to Christ's kingdom. The apostles preached the gospel through the unlimited power of the Holy Spirit and thousands upon thousands were converted by the message and joined the church, Christ's spiritual kingdom.

Rather than using the sword of the state to persecute those who rejected the gospel, the apostles were persecuted **by the state** for preaching the gospel. Paul was decapitated and Peter was crucified. James was killed with the sword (Acts 12:2) and the apostle John was exiled to the Island of

Patmos. And early Christian tradition tells us that all of the remaining apostles were martyred.

Time and again the book of Acts informs us that the apostate Jewish church attempted to use the sword of the state (the magistrates) to persecute the apostles, but nowhere in the book of Acts or in the Epistles do we ever find the church using the state to accomplish the work of Christ's kingdom. From Pentecost on the church used only one sword and that was the sword of the Spirit which is the preaching of the word of God. Their preaching brought the sword against them rather than them using the sword against others. Jesus had already predicted this when He said to His disciples:

> "'Do not think that I came to bring peace on earth. I did not come to bring peace but a sword. For I have come to 'set a man against his father, a daughter against her mother, and a daughter-in-law against her mother-in-law'; and 'a man's enemies will be those of his own household.'" (Matthew 10:34–36).

Nowhere in Acts do we find the followers of Jesus taking over the reins of political power to spread the gospel. Their sword was "the foolishness of preaching" the Word of God.

It is important to realize that although Jesus refused to be a temporal ruler and forbade His disciples from using the state to extend His kingdom, He did recognize the divinely ordained legitimacy of the civil power of Rome when he told Pilate:

> "You could have no power at all against Me unless it had been **given you from above**." (John 19:11). Emphasis supplied.

41

Thus we see that Jesus represented a kingdom from above which is **not of this world** and Pilate represented a kingdom **of this world** that was also given to him from above. Clearly, Jesus believed in two kingdoms but separate from one another!

It is a sobering fact that Jesus was judged and killed by an unholy alliance between the church and the state similar to the one that existed during the period of papal supremacy.

Before Jesus was delivered by the Jewish church to Pilate (the civil power) to be crucified, an inquisitorial process similar to the one that was used by the papacy against John Hus and countless others was followed by the religious leaders of the Jewish Sanhedrin. Notice what we are told in Matthew 26:57:

> *"And those who had laid hold of Jesus led Him away to Caiaphas the **high priest**, where the **scribes** and the **elders** were assembled." Emphasis supplied.*

After Jesus was examined by the inquisition and had been accused by false witnesses He was convicted of heresy and was adjudged worthy of death by the religious leaders (Matthew 26:66). But the church hierarchy on its own could not execute the death penalty. How, then, could they fulfill their purpose to execute the sentence of death against Jesus?

The answer is that the Jewish Sanhedrin (the church of that day) took Jesus before Pilate (the state). While they had every intention of executing the death penalty, as a church they had no authority to do so—the sword of the civil government was in the hands of Pilate.

> *"When morning came, all the chief priests and elders of the people plotted against Jesus to put Him to death. And when they had bound Him, they led Him away*

*and **delivered Him to Pontius Pilate the governor.***"
(Matthew 27:1, 2). Emphasis supplied.

In a certain rudimentary way Pilate recognized the existence of two separate kingdoms when he said to the Jewish leaders:

*"You take Him and judge Him according to **your law**
[God's law]." (John 18:31). Emphasis supplied.*

Thus Pilate, perhaps inadvertently, recognized that there were two kingdoms with two separate laws. He realized that the Jews had the law of their God and that he had the civil law of Rome.

But then the church leaders said to Pilate: *"It is not lawful for us to put anyone to death." (John 18:36)* The church needed the help of the state in order to slay Jesus!

Remarkably, Pilate publicly announced several times that Jesus had committed no crime against the Roman State and yet he condemned Jesus to death at the instigation of the Jewish church (John 18:38; 9:4, 6). In this way Pontius Pilate became the sword in the hand of the Jewish church.

And why did Pilate deliver an innocent man to death? Simply because he was afraid of losing the support of the people and thus his political position:

*"From then on Pilate sought to release Him, but the Jews cried out, saying, "If you let this Man go, **you are not Caesar's friend**. Whoever makes himself a king **speaks against Caesar**." (John 19:12). Emphasis supplied.*

After Jesus resurrected Lazarus from the dead some time earlier (John 11), the religious leaders of the Jewish church had made up their minds that He must die. In a special session of the Sanhedrin the supreme pontiff, Caiaphas, explained that the death of Jesus was necessary for the survival of their nation. This appeared to be a very patriotic reason. Said Caiaphas:

> *"You know nothing at all, nor do you consider that it is expedient for us that one man should die for the people, and not that the **whole nation should perish**." (John 11:49, 50). Emphasis supplied.*

Ironically, the very Roman sword that the Jewish church used to kill Jesus in order to save the nation was later used to destroy that very nation. In other words, instead of saving the nation, the condemnation and crucifixion of Jesus led to national apostasy and that apostasy led to national ruin. In the year 70 the very Romans whom the Jewish leaders had used to condemn Jesus now came and surrounded Jerusalem and crucified more than one million Jews outside the city. Thus what they tried to prevent by using the sword of Rome came against them by that very sword—what they tried to prevent they actually caused!!

History of the United States

Now the question must be asked: What kingdom arose around 1798 when the first beast received its deadly wound which in its founding documents explicitly recognized the legitimate simultaneous existence of two kingdoms in one nation such as Jesus believed in? The answer is unmistakable and irrefutable. States Ellen White:

> *"What nation of the New World was in 1798 rising into power, giving promise of strength and greatness, and attracting the attention of the world? The application of the symbol admits of **no question. One** nation, and **only one**, meets the specifications of this prophecy; it*

44

*points **unmistakably** to the United States of America."*
The Great Controversy, p. 440. Emphasis supplied.

The history of the United States can be divided into two great periods:

- The **Colonial** period (1620–1776)

- The **Constitutional** period (1776 to the present)

The constitutional fathers (men such as George Washington, Thomas Jefferson, John Adams, James Madison and Benjamin Franklin) of the United States knew full well three things:

- The history of the church in the middle ages

- The history of the church in the colonial period

- Their Bibles

They knew the history of the middle ages. In fact, they were living in the closing years of the 1,260 year prophecy. It is sobering to realize that the *Declaration of Independence*, the *Constitution* and the *Bill of Rights* were all written and ratified just before the deadly wound was given to the papacy in 1798.

The constitutional fathers knew that when church and state are joined together the inevitable result is the denial of civil and religious rights and persecution. They knew all about the mechanism of the Inquisition and were well acquainted with the martyrdom of holy men such as John Hus. They knew that he was held in prison for months without due process, that he was accused by false witnesses, that he had broken no civil laws, that he was tried only for the religious convictions of his conscience, that he was judged by the leaders of the church in similar fashion that the Sanhedrin had judged Jesus, that the religious leaders pronounced upon him the death penalty and that the church finally appealed to the civil power of Emperor Sigismund to ratify their death decree.

The constitutional fathers also had a first hand knowledge of the history of the colonial period. They were well aware of the fact that atheists, Jews, Quakers, Baptists and others were deprived of their civil rights simply because their beliefs and practices did not square with those of the established religion of the colonies.

They knew about Sunday laws that compelled people to attend church on pain of fines, whipping, incarceration, and in the case of the Virginia Sunday Law of 1610, death!

They knew that only members of the established church could serve in positions of the civil government and that as a result the church was corrupted by a class of hypocrites who joined the church for mercenary reasons. They knew that people's taxes were used by the government to remunerate the pastors of the established churches.

They knew full well about how Roger Williams was banished from the Massachusetts Bay Colony for teaching a strict separation of church and state. They knew how he had to flee to Rhode Island in late 1635 and early 1636 in the dead of winter in order to escape the wrath of the religious leaders.

And the Constitutional fathers knew their Bibles as well. They knew all about the trial, sentencing and execution of Jesus in the gospels.

The founding documents of the United States are remarkable indeed. In 1776 the *Declaration of Independence* affirmed that all men are created equal and that they have certain inalienable rights among which are life, liberty and the pursuit of happiness. In 1787 the *Constitution* was ratified giving the people the right to govern themselves through their representatives and in 1791 the *Bill of Rights* (the first ten amendments to the Constitution) was approved.

All this happened immediately before the papacy received its deadly wound. God, in His providence, was preparing the next world super power to appear on the stage even as the first power was about to fall.

An examination of the writings of the constitutional fathers reveals that they believed in the existence of two kingdoms in the United States that were to forever remain separate. The church was to use the spiritual sword of the Spirit to persuade through the preaching of the Word while the state was to use the material sword to preserve the civil order.

The new nation was established upon **two great principles**:

- **Republicanism** (representative civil government)
- **Protestantism** (representative religious government)

During the Middle Ages all civil matters were decided and imposed by the **king** and all religious matters were decided and enforced by the **pope**. The power flowed from above downward. When the king spoke in civil matters and the pope spoke in religious matters, the people were simply expected to obey.

The constitutional fathers established a revolutionary system of government that turned things upside down; a system where the power flowed from **below upward**—a government of the people, by the people and for the people in which people could enjoy full civil and religious liberty. The foundational idea behind this concept was that of two kingdoms in one nation, each with its own sword.

This was one of the most revolutionary experiments in human history. Ellen White describes the contrast between the system of the middle ages and the system that the constitutional fathers finally adopted and implemented:

"Among the Christian exiles who first fled to America and sought an asylum from **royal oppression** *[an oppressive state] and* **priestly intolerance** *[an oppressive church] were many who determined to establish a government upon the broad foundation of* **civil** *[state] and* **religious** *[church]* **liberty***. Their views found place in the Declaration of Independence, which sets forth the great truth that "all men are created equal" and endowed with the inalienable right to "life, liberty, and the pursuit of happiness." And the Constitution guarantees to the people the right of* **self-government,** *providing that representatives elected by the popular vote shall enact and administer the laws.* **Freedom of religious faith** *was also granted, every man being permitted to worship God according to the dictates of his conscience.* **Republicanism** *[a state without a king] and* **Protestantism** *[a church without a pope] became the fundamental principles of the nation. These principles are the* **secret of its power and prosperity***."* The Great Controversy, *p. 441. Emphasis supplied.*

Did you get that? Contrary to what most people think, the secret of the power and prosperity of the United States is not found in its vast territorial extension, its abundant natural resources, its incomparable military power, the incredible ingenuity and creativeness of its people or its abundant financial potential. Pure and simple, the retention of its power and prosperity depends on its faithfulness to its foundational principles. Remove those principles and the nation will collapse.

The United States can only expect to see things go from bad to worse as long as Protestants dabble with the papacy by seeking to unite church and state. With a clarion call we have been forewarned:

> *"When Protestant churches shall unite with the secular power to sustain a false religion, for opposing which their ancestors endured the fiercest persecution, then will the papal sabbath be enforced by the combined authority of church and state. There will be a national apostasy, which will end only in national ruin."* <u>Evangelism</u>, p. 235.

In another place Ellen White, who was born only 29 years after the deadly wound and just 36 years after the signing of the Bill of Rights, explained the providential origin and destiny of the United States:

> *"The greatest and most favored nation upon the earth is the United States. A gracious Providence has shielded this country, and poured upon her the choicest of Heaven's blessings. Here the persecuted and oppressed have found refuge. Here the Christian faith in its purity has been taught. This people have been the recipients of great light and unrivaled mercies."*

But sadly Ellen White continues:

> *"But these gifts have been repaid by ingratitude and forgetfulness of God. The Infinite One keeps a reckoning with the nations, and their guilt is proportioned to the light rejected. A fearful record now stands in the register of Heaven against our land; but the crime which shall fill up the measure of her iniquity is that of making void the law of God."* <u>4SP</u> 398.

Regarding the ideals of the founders Ellen White explained:

> *"The founders of the nation wisely sought to guard against the employment of **secular power** on the **part of the church**, with its inevitable result—intolerance and persecution." The Great Controversy, p. 442. Emphasis supplied.*

Thus the founding fathers established a government that returned to the view of church and state that had characterized Jesus and the earliest church. But we have been warned that the principles that have made this nation great will be repudiated and papal principles will be embraced.

Citizens of Two Kingdoms

When I am lecturing on this subject I customarily ask the question: To how many kingdoms do Christians belong?

The fact is that Christians are citizens of two kingdoms. They are citizens of an earthly kingdom by birth and they are citizens of the heavenly kingdom by the new birth. We have an earthly passport that identifies our earthly country of origin and we have a heavenly passport, the blood of the Lamb, which identifies us as citizens of Christ's heavenly kingdom, the church. And as citizens of both kingdoms we are commanded by Jesus to obey the legitimate civil laws of the state as well as the spiritual laws of the church that are based on a "thus says the Lord."

It has become fashionable today for Christian activists to say that separation of church and state was established only to protect the rights of the church from the encroachment of the state but just the opposite is true. The history of the middle ages and the colonial period shows beyond any doubt that the greater danger is for the church to try and use the state to sustain its teachings and accomplish its mission.

Frequently these same Christian activists will say that separation of church and state appears nowhere in the Constitution. This is true if we mean that the actual expression: *"separation of church and state"* is not in the Constitution. But, although the specific expression is not found in the Constitution, the concept is clearly and explicitly contained in the first amendment to the Constitution:

> *"Congress shall make no law respecting an **establishment of religion** [clause #1], or prohibiting the **free exercise thereof** [clause #2]; or abridging the freedom of speech, or of the press; or the right of the people peaceably to assemble, and to petition the Government for a redress of grievances [clause #3]." Emphasis supplied.*

Some contemporary Christian activists have even gone so far as to say that the first amendment applies to the federal government but does not apply to the states. But this idea has been overturned consistently in the last few decades by the Supreme Court.

Notice that the intent of the first amendment is not to forbid the establishment of <u>a</u> church in preference to other churches or <u>a</u> religion above other religions. The word 'religion' in the first amendment is not preceded by a definite or an indefinite article.

Clearly, the first amendment forbids the establishment of <u>religion period</u>. In this sense the Constitution clearly contains the concept of the separation of church and state because the state is forbidden to make laws that establish religion or prohibit its free exercise. Thus the state can have nothing to do with religion except to protect everyone's right to practice it freely according to the dictates of their own conscience.

James Madison, who is called the 'Father of the Constitution,' expressed his views on the proper relationship between religion and government:

*"There is **not a shadow of right** in the general government to intermeddle with religion. Its **least interference** with it would be a most flagrant usurpation. I can appeal to my uniform conduct on this subject that I have warmly supported religious freedom." Emphasis supplied.*

In 1797, the year before the deadly wound was given to the Roman Catholic papacy, president George Washington signed into law the *Treaty of Tripoli* which unambiguously stated:

*"The Government of the United States is **not in any sense** founded upon the Christian religion." Emphasis supplied.*

Some three years later in 1802, in a letter addressed to the Danbury Baptist Association, Thomas Jefferson expressed his understanding of the first two clauses of the first amendment by using the metaphor of the wall which he most likely borrowed from Roger Williams:

"Believing with you [the Danbury Baptists] that religion is a matter which lies solely between Man and his God, that he owes account to none other for his faith or his worship, that the legitimate powers of government reach actions only, and not opinions, I contemplate with sovereign reverence that act of the whole American people which declared that their legislature should "make no law respecting an establishment of religion, or prohibiting the free exercise thereof," thus

building a wall of separation between Church and State." Emphasis supplied.

A few years ago, the late Chief Justice of the United States Supreme Court, William Rehnquist sought to reinterpret the meaning of the Establishment Clause by affirming that it merely *"forbade the establishment of a **national religion** and forbade **preference** among religious sects and denominations."* But that it did not *"prohibit the federal government from providing **non-discriminatory** aid to religion."* Quoted in Clifford Goldstein, The Day of the Dragon, p. 79. Emphasis supplied.

Certainly Thomas Jefferson knew far better the intent of the first amendment than those who now boldly attempt to rewrite or reinterpret it.

And this separation is the best arrangement for both the church and the state. Ellen White made this telling statement that should remain etched forever in the minds of those who think they need the aid of the state to moralize America:

> *"The union of the church with the state, be the degree never so slight, while it may appear to bring the world nearer to the church, does in reality but bring the church nearer to the world."* The Great Controversy, p. 297

It will be noticed that the **third clause** of the first amendment guarantees full civil rights—freedom of speech, freedom of the press, freedom of assembly and freedom to petition the government for a redress of grievances.

Thus, encased in the first amendment to the Constitution of the **one nation,** the United States, are the **two** horns like a lamb—civil and religious liberty. And these principles of civil and religious liberty in turn are based on the foundational idea that the kingdom of the church and the kingdom of the state should be kept separate. When either of the first two clauses of the first amendment is violated by the government, the inevitable result is the loss of the civil liberties guaranteed by the third clause and inevitably persecution.

Much is being said today in Evangelical circles about the need for Americans to be patriotic and Christian. It is assumed that in order to be both, the United States government must support religion through things like vouchers, school prayer, federal funds for charitable choice, religious displays on public property, Ten Commandment monuments in our courtrooms and the like.

But as we have already seen, to separate the affairs of the church and the state is Christian because this is what Christ taught. It is also patriotic because it is in harmony with the founding documents of the nation. To join church and state would thus be antichristian (against what Christ taught) and unpatriotic (against what the founding fathers of America taught).

The Establishment Clause in Daniel 3

Daniel three and six are vivid illustrations of what happens when the first two clauses of the First Amendment are violated—the result is the loss of freedom and the ultimate civil right, life itself.

In Daniel three we find king Nebuchadnezzar attempting to **establish** religion. He raised an image and commanded all nations, tongues and peoples to worship it. Those who refused to comply with this religious decree enforced by the state were to be deprived of the ultimate civil right—life itself! Thus when the king attempted to **establish** religion this automatically led to persecution against those who failed to comply.

The three young men who refused to obey the religious law established by the civil ruler are shown elsewhere in the book to be respectful of the king's legitimate civil commands.

But when the king crossed the line between civil and religious matters they drew a line in the sand. When the civil power overstepped its legitimate bounds, the three young men chose to obey God rather than man and as a result they were condemned to the fiery furnace.

In the final instance the three young men had no human court of appeal and it looked like the king had all the cards. In fact the king defiantly raised his hand to heaven and roared: *"And what god will be able to deliver you from my hand?"*

But God was actually the final court of appeal and He personally intervened and delivered them in spectacular fashion.

The Free Exercise Clause in Daniel 6

The story of Daniel six is similar yet different. In Daniel six we see what happens when the **free exercise** clause of the First Amendment is violated. You see, in Daniel six king Darius was not establishing a religious observance but rather forbidding the free exercise to pray to whomever his subjects wished.

And this law forbidding the free exercise of religion led to the persecution of Daniel who insisted on worshiping God according to the dictates of his own conscience. Like his three friends, Daniel practiced civil disobedience because the king had overstepped his legitimate sphere of power.

Daniel was loved by the king and is seen elsewhere in the book as a loyal subject to all the legitimate civil laws of the Medes and Persians. He practiced civil disobedience only when the king overstepped his legitimate bounds. When the king crossed the line between civil and religious matters, Daniel drew a line in the sand.

On this occasion all the power once again seemed to be in the hands of the enemies of Daniel. The law of the Medes and Persians could not be changed or revoked so it appeared that Daniel was doomed to destruction. But as in the case of Daniel's three friends, God was the final court of appeal and He intervened in spectacular fashion to deliver his servant from the lions and from his enemies.

Significantly, neither Nebuchadnezzar nor Darius got the point that God was trying to teach them. After God delivered the three young men from the furnace, Nebuchadnezzar threatened that anyone who said anything against the God of Daniel would be cut in pieces and their houses razed to the ground. He didn't yet understand that God does not coerce people to embrace even true religion because true religion must spring from the heart!

And after Daniel was delivered from the lion's den king Darius made a decree that everyone was obligated to tremble and fear before the God of Daniel. Once again, the king didn't get the point. People can not be forced to tremble and fear before God—this must come from a heart that loves Him.

The First Amendment in the End Time

Someone might ask, what does all this have to do with the end time?

Ellen White has stated that the United States will eventually violate both the establishment clause and the free exercise clause of the First Amendment. It will not only compel all to keep Sunday thus establishing religion but it will also forbid the observance of the Sabbath thus forbidding the free exercise thereof. Regarding this she states:

*"The time will come when men will not only **forbid Sunday work**, but they will try to **force men to labor on the Sabbath**. And men will be asked to **renounce the Sabbath** and to **subscribe to Sunday observance***

*or forfeit their **freedom** and their **lives**. But the time for this has not yet come, for the truth must be presented more fully before the people as a witness."* <u>Maranatha,</u> *p. 177. Emphasis supplied.*

When this time comes, the apostasy that **was begun** when the papacy changed the day of worship from Sabbath to Sunday during the 1,260 years (Daniel 7:25) will be **completed** by apostate Protestantism at the end of time when it enforces the mark of the beast.

Sadly the process will have come full circle. Just as the papacy destroyed the apostolic view of church and state, so apostate Protestantism will overturn the view of church and state that was established and taught the founding fathers of the United States.

Aren't Sunday Laws Unconstitutional?

The key question is this: Wouldn't the establishment of Sunday by congress as the national day of rest be a clear violation of the establishment clause of the first amendment and thus unconstitutional?

And a related question: Wouldn't a congressional law forbidding the observance of the Sabbath also be in violation of the free exercise clause of the first amendment and thus also unconstitutional? The answer of any rational person to these questions would be yes.

I am quite sure that when that time comes the constitutionality of such laws will be questioned not only by Seventh-day Adventists but also by organizations such as the ACLU. According to Bible prophecy the appeal will fall upon deaf ears—there will be no redress of grievances.

We are not to expect the eradication of the first amendment from the Constitution. What will most likely happen is that the Supreme Court will declare, most likely in a time of dire national emergency, that unconstitutional laws are constitutional. After all, we are not told that the two lamb-like horns will be broken before the land beast speaks as a dragon. It will still have the two horns like a lamb while it speaks like a dragon.

Three Branches of Government

Our system of government like that of many other nations has three branches: The executive, the legislative and the judicial. As we all know, the legislative branch writes the laws, the executive branch enforces the laws and the judicial interprets them. I frequently ask people: Which of these three branches is the most powerful? The answer is usually, the executive.

But actually the most powerful branch of government in the United States is the judicial, particularly the Supreme Court. And why is this? The answer is quite simple. Congress can write a bill but if the Supreme Court declares it unconstitutional the bill will not become law. The flip side is also true: Congress could draw up a bill that is clearly unconstitutional but if the Supreme Court declares it constitutional it would be enforced.

If you don't think that the Supreme Court is the most powerful branch of government, just remember what happened in the 2000 election. After many appeals to various courts of the land, the case was taken to the Supreme Court and when the Supreme Court spoke, George W. Bush became president and there was no more discussion.

There are now five Roman Catholics on the Supreme Court of the United States: Chief Justice John Roberts and justices Antonin Scalia, Clarence Thomas, Anthony Kennedy and Samuel Alito. There is nothing to indicate that the trend of naming Roman Catholics to the Court will end anytime soon, particularly if a conservative candidate wins the presidency. The more liberal judges on the Court are getting up in years and most likely they will be replaced in the next eight years. Can we fathom what it will be like to have seven or more Roman Catholics on the Supreme Court?

Ellen White predicted long ago what would happen if our protestant government should concede to the papacy:

> *"They [Christians] do not see that if a **Protestant government** sacrifices **the principles** that have made them a free, independent nation, and through **legislation** [this is drawn up in Congress] brings into the Constitution, principles that will propagate papal falsehood and papal delusion, they are plunging into the **Roman horrors of the Dark Ages**."* Review and Herald, December 11, 1888. Emphasis supplied.

Some Adventists say that this scenario is alarmist or sensationalist, that the Supreme Court justices are patriotic Americans and that they would never return the United States to the terrors of the dark ages.

But notice what we are told in The Great Controversy:

> *"The Roman Catholic Church, with all its ramifications throughout the world, forms one vast organization under the control, and designed to serve the interests, of the papal see. Its millions of communicants, in every country on the globe, are instructed to **hold themselves as bound in allegiance to the pope**. Whatever their nationality or their government, they are to regard the **authority of the church as above all other**. Though they may take the oath pledging their loyalty to the state, yet back of this lies the **vow of obedience***

*to **Rome**, absolving them from every pledge inimical to her interests." The Great Controversy, p. 580. Emphasis supplied.*

Many Protestants today are fascinated by the papacy. They point to the papacy's fight for human rights, for the poor, for life, for morality, for conventional marriage. They believe that the papacy has changed and therefore there is nothing to fear. Yet the papacy has not repudiated its aspirations to global political power. She is harmless when she is helpless:

"It is a part of her [the papacy's] policy to assume the character which will best accomplish her purpose; but beneath the variable appearance of the chameleon she conceals the invariable venom of the serpent." The Great Controversy, p. 571.

Ellen White has warned about what is to come:

*"When the land which the Lord provided as an asylum for His people, that they might worship Him according to the dictates of their own consciences, the land over which for long years the shield of Omnipotence has been spread, the land which God has favored by making it the depository of the pure religion of Christ—when that land shall, **through its legislators** [it will be done by Congress], abjure the principles of Protestantism, and give countenance to Romish apostasy in tampering with God's law—it is then that the final work of the man of sin will be revealed. **Protestants** will throw their **whole influence and strength** on the side of the Papacy; by a **national act** [this is an act of Congress] enforcing the false sabbath, they will give **life** and **vig-***

*or [help the wound to heal by giving the sword back]
to the corrupt faith of Rome, **reviving** [giving her life
again so she must have been wounded] her tyranny
and oppression of conscience. Then it will be time for
God to work in mighty power for the vindication of His
truth." Maranatha, p. 179. Emphasis supplied.*

Then the United States will have formed a **mirror reflection** [image] of the papacy **in its honor**. The sea beast (the papacy) was characterized by a church that employed the power of the state to punish dissenters and so it will be with the land beast that makes the image.

*"In order for the United States to form an image of the
beast, the religious power must **so control the civil
government** that the authority of the state will also be
employed by the church to accomplish her own ends."
The Great Controversy, p. 443. Emphasis supplied.*

*"When the leading churches of the United States, **uniting upon such points of doctrine as are held by them
in common,** shall **influence the state** to enforce their
decrees and to sustain their institutions, then Protestant
America will have formed an image of the Roman hierarchy, and the **infliction of civil penalties** upon dissenters will inevitably result." The Great Controversy, p.
445. Emphasis supplied.*

We are told in Revelation 13:11 that the land beast will speak like a dragon, that is, like Satan through Rome. The question is: How does the United States speak? The answer is that it speaks through its duly elected representatives in congress.

Explains Ellen White:

*"The 'speaking' of the nation is the action of its **legislative** and **judicial** authorities. By such action it will give the lie to those liberal and peaceful principles which it has put forth as the foundation of its policy." The Great Controversy, p. 442. Emphasis supplied.*

During the first stage of its dominion the sea beast of Revelation 13 (the papacy) thought it could change the law of God by changing the day of worship from Sabbath to Sunday. The land beast (the United States) will enforce this change by using the sword of the state. The whole world will then be led to follow the example of the United States.

*"As America, the land of religious liberty, shall unite with the papacy in forcing the conscience and compelling men to honor the false sabbath, the people of **every country on the globe** will be led to follow her example" Testimonies for the Church, volume 6, p. 18. Emphasis supplied.*

How this can happen when the reputation of the United States in the world at present is at such a low ebb remains to be seen. But there can be little doubt that it will take place in the midst of a cataclysmic and catastrophic chain of events such as a global economic collapse, unparalleled natural disasters, unheard of crime and spectacular communications from the spirit world (perhaps impersonating Mary and John Paul II) as to what to do about these problems.

The issue will then be global survival. The argument used anciently by Caiaphas will be used once more: *"It is better for these dissenters to die than for the United States to perish."*

This argument will appear patriotic and Christian but it will prove to be just the opposite. Like with the Jewish nation, national apostasy will be followed speedily by national ruin.

The Spirit of Prophecy has warned us about the danger of closing our eyes to the dangers ahead:

> "Protestants have **tampered with** and **patronized** popery; they have made **compromises** and **concessions** which papists themselves are surprised to see and fail to understand. Men are **closing their eyes** to the real character of Romanism, and the dangers to be apprehended from her supremacy. The people need to be aroused to resist the advances of this most dangerous foe to **civil and religious liberty**." The Great Controversy, p. 566. Emphasis supplied.

On a church level recent decades have seen a growing intimacy between the Protestant churches in the United States and the Roman Catholic papacy. Enthusiastic cooperation on social issues such as abortion and gay marriage has given them a common agenda. Cooperation in the election of conservative candidates has given them a common cause. Prominent Catholic and Evangelical leaders in 1992 signed the document, Evangelicals and Catholics Together and Lutherans and Catholics in 1999 signed the Joint Declaration on Righteousness by Faith. Most Protestants are oblivious to the dangers presented by the papacy because they have forgotten history. And those who fail to learn from the mistakes of history are bound to repeat them.

An example of this growing intimacy between Protestants and the papacy can be seen by the ecumenical meeting that was held at St. Joseph's church in Manhattan, New York, on Friday, April 18, 2008. No less than 250 leaders from the great mainline Protestant denominations and other Christian organizations in the United States participated including United Methodists, Evangelical Lutherans, Lutheran Church Missouri Synod, the National Association of Evangelicals,

Presbyterians, the Reformed church, the National Baptist Convention, various Pentecostal groups, Greek Orthodox, Armenian, Episcopalian. Even the Mormons were represented! Fifteen of these leaders were chosen to personally shake the pope's hand.

Benedict XVI stood at the front of the church in his white papal robe and cassock as each of these fifteen representatives came forward to cordially shake his hand; some of them inclining their head to him and all of them uttering kind words. This, in spite of the fact that Benedict has explicitly said that Protestant churches are not true Christian churches. So to speak, Martin Luther must have been rolling over in his grave at such a betrayal of the Protestant Reformation that cost so much sweat, blood and tears!

Building upon the contacts that John Paul II had made with Judaism, earlier in the day Benedict XVI had visited the Park East Synagogue in New York City where he was cordially received by Rabbi Arthur Schneier and where they exchanged gifts. Both seemed to be willing to bury the past and this in spite of the fact that Schneier lived under Nazi occupation in Budapest during World War II while Joseph Ratzinger belonged to the Hitler Youth as a boy. How times have changed!

Ellen White has warned:

"The Roman Church now presents a fair front to the world, covering with apologies her record of horrible cruelties. She has clothed herself in Christlike garments; but she is unchanged. Every principle of the papacy that existed in past ages exists today. The doctrines devised in the darkest ages are still held. Let none deceive themselves. The papacy that Protestants are now so ready to honor is the same that ruled the world in the days

of the Reformation, when men of God stood up, at the peril of their lives, to expose her iniquity. She possesses the same pride and arrogant assumption that lorded it over kings and princes, and claimed the prerogatives of God. Her spirit is no less cruel and despotic now than when she crushed out human liberty and slew the saints of the Most High." GC 571.

Protestant leaders have undoubtedly been impressed by John Paul's and Benedict's talk about the culture of life, the dignity of the human person, the opposition to the death penalty and the sanctity of human life. Even Billy Graham more than once has affirmed that John Paul II was the greatest moral voice in the world. This talk has lulled Protestantism to sleep and the awakening will be rude indeed!

Dr. Ralph Reed who was the president of the Christian Coalition in its heyday once stated: "The truth my friends is this. Catholicism never has been, is not today, and never will be a threat to American democracy. It was and remains the most colorful and the most vibrant thread running through the tapestry of American democracy." (Quoted in G. Edward Reid, Sunday's Coming, p. 72).

What an inexcusable blindness! Is Ralph Reed un-aware of the papacy's past track record? Is he so caught up in the wave of ecumenical activism that he actually believes that the papacy has changed and now cares about civil and religious liberty?

On a state level, the United States government has also shown a growing infatuation with the papacy. From Ronald Reagan and John Paul II teaming up to overthrow the former Soviet Union, to establishing diplomatic relations with the Holy See, to congress giving John Paul II the Congressional Medal of Freedom, to George W. Bush's regular consultations with the Catholic bishops, to three presidents, a president's wife, and a secretary of State bowing before the casket of John Paul II in Rome, to the pope visiting the White House, to George W. Bush selecting two conservative Roman Catholics for the Supreme Court, there has been a incredible miasma of historical amnesia about the dangers presented by the papacy.

A Repetition of History

We have been warned that unscrupulous and self-serving legislators, like Pilate, in order to retain their political position and influence, will give in to the popular demand for a national Sunday law and will eventually condemn God's faithful children to death:

> "To secure popularity and patronage [votes], legislators will yield to the demand for a Sunday law." Testimonies for the Church, volume 4, p. 451.

> "Plans of serious import to the people of God are advancing in an underhand manner among the clergymen of various denominations, and the object of this secret maneuvering is to win popular favor for the enforcement of Sunday sacredness. If the people can be led to favor a Sunday law, then the clergy intend to exert their united influence to obtain a religious amendment to the Constitution, and compel the nation to keep Sunday." Review and Herald, December 24, 1889.

When Pilate offered to release Jesus in place of Barabbas the populace clamored for Pilate rather to release Barabbas. And who instigated the multitudes to clamor for the release of Barabbas? Notice the answer in Mark 15:11:

*"But the **chief priests stirred up the crowd**, so that he should rather release Barabbas to them." Emphasis supplied.*

It was the ministers of that day and age who instigated the multitudes to cry out for the blood of Jesus. The initiative came from the religious leaders, not from the state or from the populace. Are we to expect anything different in the end time?

An illustration of this maneuvering by the clergy can be seen in a statement that was made by **Mike Huckabee**, a Baptist minister and presidential primary candidate for the Republican Party in the year 2008. In a sermon he gave at a church in Warren, Michigan on the eve of the Michigan primary he stated:

*"I have opponents in this race who do not want to **change the Constitution** but I believe it's a lot easier to **change the Constitution** than it would be to change the word of the living God and that's what we need to do is to **amend the Constitution** so that its in **God's standards**, rather than change God's standards so that it lines up with some contemporary view of how we treat each other and how we treat the family."*

In all fairness to Mr. Huckabee he was talking about amending the Constitution to outlaw gay marriage and abortion. But notice that his proposed amendment to the Constitution would have religious/biblical reasons rather than secular ones! His reason for amending the Constitution would be to put it in line with the Word of the living God. This would be a clear infringement of the first amendment.

The question is: How long would it be until Mr. Huckabee along with other clergy would propose a national Sunday law as well in order to make the Constitution fall in line with what they understand to be God's day of rest? Does he believe any less that Sunday is God's day of rest than he does that abortion and gay marriage should be illegal?

In a CNN interview with Wolf Blitzer on Sunday, April 20, 2008, Mr. Huckabee, a stanch Southern Baptist, went on the record stating that he is a great admirer of John Paul II and Benedict XVI and called them great spiritual leaders. Both popes have unabashedly stated that Sunday observance should be guaranteed by civil legislation. When that day comes, would Mr. Huckabee disagree with them?

Ellen White has vividly described what will happen to God's people when the Sunday law is being agitated:

> *"Those who honor the Bible Sabbath will be denounced as **enemies of law and order**, as breaking down the moral restraints of society, causing anarchy and corruption, and calling down the judgments of God upon the earth. Their conscientious scruples will be pronounced obstinacy, stubbornness, and **contempt of authority**. They will be accused of **disaffection toward the government**. Ministers who deny the obligation of the divine law will present from the pulpit the duty of **yielding obedience to the civil authorities as ordained of God**. In **legislative halls** and **courts of justice**, commandment keepers will be misrepresented and condemned. A false coloring will be given to their words; the worst construction will be put upon their motives."*
> The Great Controversy, p. 592. Emphasis supplied.

Lessons from the Earliest Church

When the early church lost the Spirit and power of the true gospel, the moral condition of the empire quickly deteriorated. The church leaders seeing that morality was at such a low point linked up with the state to force people to be moral and the result was the papacy which used the sword of the civil power to punish dissenters.

The prophecy of Revelation 13:11–18 indicates that Protestantism in the United States will make an image of this. Protestantism has lost the Spirit and power of the true gospel; it has preached for so long that Christians are no longer required to keep the law because they are under grace that the people have come to believe it and the consequences can be clearly seen in a decaying society.

As Protestants have seen things going from bad to worse in American society they have once again begun to emphasize the need to keep the Ten Commandments. But their solution to society's problems is to have the civil government enforce morality through legislation or constitutional amendments. Thus they would have the civil government fix what they themselves have created by preaching an unbalanced view of law and grace. Christian activists today blame what they call a secular humanist government for the steady decline in morality when a good share of the blame lies at their own doorstep.

Many Protestants have come to believe that by having "*In God we Trust*" on our currency, or by reciting "one nation under God" in the Pledge of Allegiance, or by mandating prayer in public schools, or by posting the Ten Commandments in our courtrooms or by putting Christmas displays on public property, or by enacting a constitutional amendment against gay marriage, the nation will be brought back to God. The time is coming when everyone who does not agree will be accused of causing the corruption and immorality that are bringing down the high judgments of God.

Seventh-day Adventists have frequently been accused by Protestants of being legalists because they emphasize that God requires His children to faithfully keep the Sabbath. But there is no greater legalism than forcing people to keep Sunday on pain of civil penalties.

Protestantism has forgotten that its real source of power is found in preaching and practicing the unadulterated Word of God through the ministration of the Holy Spirit. It has instead emphasized a prosperity gospel, a gospel of signs and wonders, a gospel of psychological self-help and a gospel of political involvement. It has thus lost its power and sees government as the way to solve the problem.

In a rather lengthy statement Ellen White compares the condition of the United States in her day with the crying abuses that existed in the ancient Roman Empire in the days of Christ:

> *"But today in the religious world there are multitudes who, as they believe, are working for the establishment of the kingdom of Christ as an **earthly and temporal dominion**. They desire to make our Lord the **ruler of the kingdoms of this world**, the ruler in **its courts and camps**, its **legislative halls**, its **palaces** and **market places**. They expect Him to rule through **legal enactments**, enforced by human authority. Since Christ is not now here in person, they themselves will undertake to act in His stead, to **execute the laws of His kingdom**. The establishment of such a kingdom is what the Jews desired in the days of Christ. They would have received Jesus, had He been willing to establish a temporal dominion, to enforce what they regarded as the laws of God, and to make them the expositors of His will and the agents of His authority. But He said, 'My kingdom*

70

is not of this world.' John 18:36. He would not accept the earthly throne.

"The government under which Jesus lived was corrupt and oppressive; on every hand were crying abuses,— extortion, intolerance, and grinding cruelty. Yet the Savior attempted **no civil reforms.** *He attacked no national abuses, nor condemned the national enemies. He did not interfere with the authority or administration of those in power. He who was our example kept* **aloof from earthly governments.** *Not because He was indifferent to the woes of men, but because the remedy did not lie in merely human and external measures. To be efficient, the cure must reach men individually, and must regenerate the heart.*

"Not by the decisions of courts or councils or legislative assemblies, not by the patronage of worldly great men, is the kingdom of Christ established, but by the implanting of Christ's nature in humanity through the work of the Holy Spirit. 'As many as received Him, to them gave He power to become the sons of God, even to them that believe on His name: which were born, not of blood, nor of the will of the flesh, nor of the will of man, but of God.' John 1:12, 13. Here is the only power that can work the uplifting of mankind. And the human agency for the accomplishment of this work is the teaching and practicing of the word of God." The Desire of Ages, pp. 509, 510. Emphasis supplied.

When church and state are fully joined together in unholy matrimony, and I believe this is even at the door, then the only and final court of appeal for the saints will be God. Ellen

White assures us that even legislators and judges will refuse to hear our arguments in favor of the Sabbath because they know that they are irrefutable. Yet we have been assured:

> *"When the law of God has been made void, and apostasy becomes a national sin, the Lord will work in behalf of His people. Their extremity will be His opportunity. He will manifest His power in behalf of His church. ..."* <u>3SM</u> *388.*

Then the same story will be repeated with the United States as happened with the Jewish nation. National apostasy will be followed speedily by national ruin.

The Perspective of Revelation 17

Revelation 17 presents a vivid portrayal of the time when the prophecy of Revelation 13:11–18 will be fulfilled. In this passage we see a harlot woman whose name is Babylon (17:5) who sits on many waters, that is, upon nations, multitudes, tongues and people (17:1, 15). She sustains an adulterous spiritual relationship with the kings of the earth (17:2). She is garbed in purple and scarlet, gold and precious stones (17:4). The kings of the world gladly drink her fermented wine of false doctrine (17:2) and give decrees against those who refuse to drink with them. She has daughters that were born from her at some point because she is called the 'mother of harlots' (17:5). And most significantly, she sheds the blood of the saints and the martyrs of Jesus (17:6).

We are told that for a while the kings of the earth will do her bidding and that of her daughters. But at the climactic moment when she appears to be seated as queen and will not see widowhood, the kings of the earth will turn on her for they *"will hate the harlot, make her desolate and naked, eat her flesh and burn her with fire."* (17:16, 17). Thus, the sword of the kings that she used to slay the saints will finally be used by the kings to slay her.

I couldn't help but be amazed at the reception pope Benedict XVI received when he spoke before the United Nations on Friday, April 18, 2008. He entered down the center isle in his white pontifical robes to a thunderous standing ovation by the leaders of practically every nation on earth. It is obvious that the kings of the earth are oblivious to the dangers presented by this despotic system. They are playing with fire and sooner or later they will be burned.

Ellen White describes the climactic moment when the multitudes will withdraw their support from their religious leaders:

"The people see that they have been deluded. They accuse one another of having led them to destruction; but all unite in heaping their bitterest condemnation upon the ministers. Unfaithful pastors have prophesied smooth things; they have led their hearers to make void the law of God and to persecute those who would keep it holy. Now, in their despair, these teachers confess before the world their work of deception. The multitudes are filled with fury. 'We are lost!' they cry, 'and you are the cause of our ruin;' and they turn upon the false shepherds. The very ones that once admired them most will pronounce the most dreadful curses upon them. The very hands that once crowned them with laurels will be raised for their destruction. The swords which were to slay God's people are now employed to destroy their enemies. Everywhere there is strife and bloodshed." GC 655.

Another French Revolution

When the pope was taken captive in 1798 the handcuffs that had fallen off the papacy in 508 were slapped on again and the sword was removed from her hand. As a result she could no longer use the political powers and the masses to accomplish her purposes.

But prophecy tells us that the United States is the power that will unlock the cuffs and give the papacy her freedom again. And the United States will put the sword of civil power in her hand once again.

For a while the papacy allied with Protestants will seem to have the upper hand. But in the end Jesus will deliver His faithful people as he did the three young Hebrews and Daniel.

Impressive will be the moment when the kings of the earth and their subjects will turn on the Mother of harlots and her daughters. Scenes similar to the French Revolution will be repeated but on a worldwide scale.

The ancient story of Esther is a vivid illustration of what will take place on the global stage. In Esther 3:2 we are told that King Ahasuerus gave a decree that everyone in the kingdom should bow before Haman and pay him homage. Of course, Mordecai, for conscientious reasons, refused to comply with the king's command.

When Haman saw that Mordecai did not bow down and pay him homage he was filled with rage and made up his mind that Mordecai and all his people must be exterminated. He therefore went before the king and with carefully crafted arguments duped him into thinking that the Jews were a menace to the stability and security of the kingdom (Esther 3:8).

He told the king that throughout the entire realm of his rule there was a small pervasive remnant that had different laws than the Medes and Persians and therefore they did not keep the king's laws. He argued that to keep them around would lead to anarchy and dissolution of the kingdom (Esther 3:8).

Then Haman made a diabolical suggestion to the king, a suggestion that most likely had previously been made to him by his wife, Zeresh. He told him that for the survival of the kingdom he should sign a death decree authorizing the extermination of Mordecai and all his people on a specific day. The king consented and Haman drew up the dated death decree, signed it with the signet ring of the king and delivered it to be enforced in the entire kingdom (Esther 3:8, 9).

To this point in the story, the king was oblivious to the real intentions of his advisor. He truly believed that Haman was concerned with his welfare and that of his kingdom. In other words, the king implicitly trusted the counsel of his advisor.

For a while, all seemed to be going according to plan. The triumvirate composed of the king, Haman and Zeresh was all on the same page. On the thirteenth day of the month of Adar the death decree was to be executed and the nation would be rid of the thorn in Haman's side.

But at the critical moment, when there appeared to be no hope for God's people, Queen Esther stepped onto the stage and unmasked Haman's plot before the king. As a result, the king's wrath was shifted from Mordecai and his people to Haman and his wife. To make a long story short, the gallows that were built to slay Mordecai were used to slay Haman and his wife. That is to say, the very weapon that was prepared to slay God's people was used to slay their enemies.

At the end of time a story similar to this will transpire with God's spiritual worldwide Israel. An evil triumvirate composed of the harlot mother, her harlot daughters and the kings of the earth will conspire to exterminate the remnant of God.

But at the hour of the utmost extremity Christ will intervene to deliver His people by turning the multitudes and the kings of the earth against the harlot and her daughters. Thus when the king of the north goes out with great wrath to slay and annihilate many, Christ will stand up to defend His people and the king of the north will come to his end with no one to help him! (See Daniel 11:44–12:1.) Wonderful will be the spectacular deliverance of those who would rather die than disobey God!

Regarding the final alliance of apostate Protestantism and Roman Catholicism, Ellen White explained:

*"I saw that the two-horned beast had a dragon's mouth, and that his power was in his head, and that the decree would go out of his mouth. Then I saw the Mother of Harlots [the papacy]; that the mother was not the daughters [apostate Protestantism], but separate and distinct from them. She has had her day [during the 1,260 years, and **it is past,** and her daughters, the **Protestant sects,** were the **next to come on the stage** and **act out the same mind** [an image] that the mother had when she persecuted the saints. I saw that as the mother has been **declining in power** [because of the deadly wound], the **daughters had been growing,** and soon they will **exercise the power once exercised by the mother.***

*"I saw the nominal church and nominal Adventists, like Judas, would **betray us to the Catholics** to obtain their influence to come against the truth. The saints then will be an obscure people, little known to the Catholics; but the churches and nominal Adventists who know of our faith and customs (for they hated us on account of the Sabbath, for they could not refute it) **will betray the***

saints and report them to the Catholics as those who disregard the institutions of the people; that is, that they keep the Sabbath and disregard Sunday.

*"Then the **Catholics bid the Protestants** to go forward, and **issue a decree** that all who will not observe the first day of the week, instead of the seventh day, shall be slain. And the Catholics, whose numbers are large, **will stand by the Protestants**. The Catholics **will give their power to the image of the beast**. And the Protestants will work **as their mother worked before them** to destroy the saints. But before their decree bring or bear fruit, the saints will be delivered by the Voice of God." Ellen G. White, <u>Spaulding Magan Collection</u>, pp. 1, 2. Emphasis supplied.*

Why the United States?

I believe that God has raised up the United States to keep the deadly wound in place so as to make it possible for God's people to preach the three angels messages in an environment of freedom and peace. Unfortunately we have squandered much of this period of freedom and Ellen White has told us that:

*"The work which **the church has failed to do** in a time of peace and prosperity [notice the same words that Ellen White used to describe the secret of success of the United States], she will have to do in a **terrible crisis**, under most discouraging, forbidding, circumstances. **The warnings that worldly conformity has silenced or withheld must be given under the fiercest opposition from enemies of the faith.** And at that time the superficial, conservative class, whose influence has*

steadily **retarded the progress of the work**, *will re-nounce the faith, and take their stand with its avowed enemies, toward whom their sympathies have long been tending. These* **apostates** *will then manifest the* **most bitter enmity** *doing all in their power to oppress and malign their former brethren, and to excite indignation against them. This day is just before us. The members of the church will individually be tested and proved. They will be placed in circumstances where* **they will be forced to bear witness for the truth.** *Many will be called to speak before councils and in courts of justice, perhaps separately and alone.* **The experience which would have helped them in this emergency they have neglected to obtain, and their souls are burdened with remorse for wasted opportunities and neglected privileges.**" <u>Testimonies for the Church</u>, *volume 5, p. 463. Emphasis supplied.*

God's Final Call

God has called His remnant people to give the trumpet a certain sound. Seventh-day Adventist have been called by God to warn nations, peoples, tongues and kings (Revelation 10:11) about the imminent dangers ahead. We are to warn in no uncertain tones about the dangers represented by the harlot and her daughters. In fact, our mission is to call God's faithful children out of these apostate religious systems to join the remnant of God.

"After these things I saw another angel coming down from heaven, having great authority, and the earth was illuminated with his glory. And he cried mightily with a loud voice, saying, "Babylon the great is fallen, is fallen, and has become a dwelling place of demons,

*a prison for every foul spirit, and a cage for every unclean and hated bird! For all the nations have drunk of the wine of the wrath of her fornication, the kings of the earth have committed fornication with her, and the merchants of the earth have become rich through the abundance of her luxury." And I heard another voice from heaven saying, "**Come out of her, my people**, lest you share in her sins, and lest you receive of her plagues. For her sins have reached to heaven, and God has remembered her iniquities."*

God has multitudes of faithful children who belong to the various churches represented by the harlot and her daughters. God has called Seventh-day Adventists to give a clarion call for these true children to come out and join the remnant who keep the commandments of God and have the testimony of Jesus.

Yet political correctness, false charity, and peer pressure have frequently muted the Seventh-day Adventist trumpet. Rather than calling God's faithful children out of Babylon we have been desirous of embracing the theology, lifestyle and worship style of Babylon.

Will you, dear Seventh-day Adventist Christian, answer God's call to shout God's end time message from the rooftops? Will you be willing, even at the risk of all, to enlist in God's army to war against Satan's kingdom?

And will you, dear child of God in Babylon, answer God's call and come out of Babylon to join those who keep the commandments of God and the faith of Jesus? The decision is yours and it will determine your eternal destiny!

About Pastor Stephen Bohr

Pastor Bohr loves the Lord with all his heart. He is committed to working for Him with all his mind, soul and might. He has dedicated years to the study of the prophetic message of the Bible.

He is best known for his groundbreaking video series, "Cracking the Genesis Code." He is a regular presenter on the **3ABN** TV network.

Pastor Bohr teaches "Foundations of Seventh-day Adventist Theology" at the Amazing Facts College of Evangelism. Presently he serves as senior pastor of Fresno Central Seventh-day Adventist Church and also as speaker for **Secrets Unsealed**, an organization committed to the preservation, proclamation and proliferation of the present truth message of the Seventh-day Adventist Church.

Secrets Unsealed is a non-profit supporting ministry based out of Fresno, California. We are located at the Fresno Central Seventh-day Adventist Church. If you would like to visit us, go to our web site for driving directions to our offices. If you would just like to write us, please use our mailing address.

Secrets Unsealed • 1-559-264-2300
PO Box 6545 Fresno, CA 93703-6545
E-mail: info@secretsunsealed.org
www.secretsunsealed.org

Check out our online catalog filled with great books, videos, CDs, articles, Bible study materials, and more! Be sure to sign up for our free newsletter.